Silver Burdett Ginn Science
DISCOVERYWORKS

Silver Burdett Ginn

Parsippany, NJ   Needham, MA

Atlanta, GA   Deerfield, IL   Irving, TX   Upland, CA

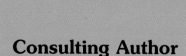

Authors

William Badders
Science Resource Teacher
Cleveland Public Schools
Cleveland, OH

Lowell J. Bethel
Professor of Science Education
The University of Texas at Austin
Austin, TX

Victoria Fu
Professor of Child Development
Virginia Polytechnic Institute and
State University
Blacksburg, VA

Donald Peck
Director, Center for Elementary Science
Fairleigh Dickinson University
Madison, NJ

Carolyn Sumners
Director of Astronomy and Physics
Houston Museum of Natural Science
Houston, TX

Catherine Valentino
Senior Vice President for
Curriculum Development
Voyager Expanded Learning
West Kingston, RI

Consulting Author

R. Mike Mullane
Astronaut, retired
Albuquerque, NM

Contributing Writers

Wendy Pfeffer
Jeanne Gleason

Credits and acknowledgements appear on page H30,
which consistutes an extension of this copyright page.

Silver Burdett Ginn
A Division of Simon & Schuster
299 Jefferson Road, P.O. Box 480
Parsippany, NJ 07054-0480

ISBN 0-382-41634-1

1 2 3 4 5 6 7 8 9 10 RRD 05 04 03 02 01 00 99 98

CONTENTS

KINDS OF LIVING THINGS

Theme: Systems

Observing
Plants and Animals

WHAT YOU NEED

crayons

Science Notebook

1. Take a walk with your class. Look for plants and animals.

2. Draw the plants you see. Write or tell about where you see the plants.

3. Draw the animals you see. Write or tell about what the animals are doing.

Think! How are plants and animals different from each other?

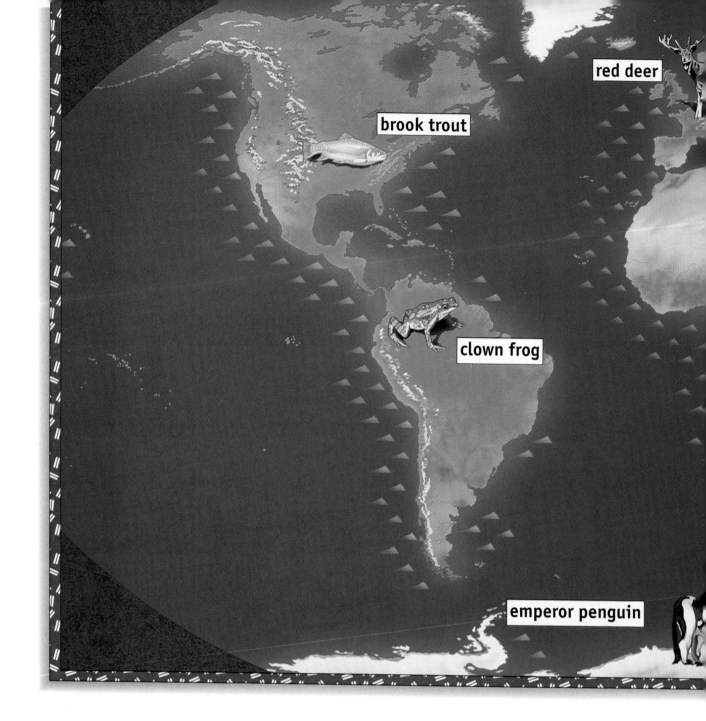

red deer

brook trout

clown frog

emperor penguin

Plants and Animals Everywhere

There are many kinds of plants and animals. They all live on the earth. You can find plants and animals almost everywhere. They live in deserts. They live in forests. They live in oceans. They even live in your home.

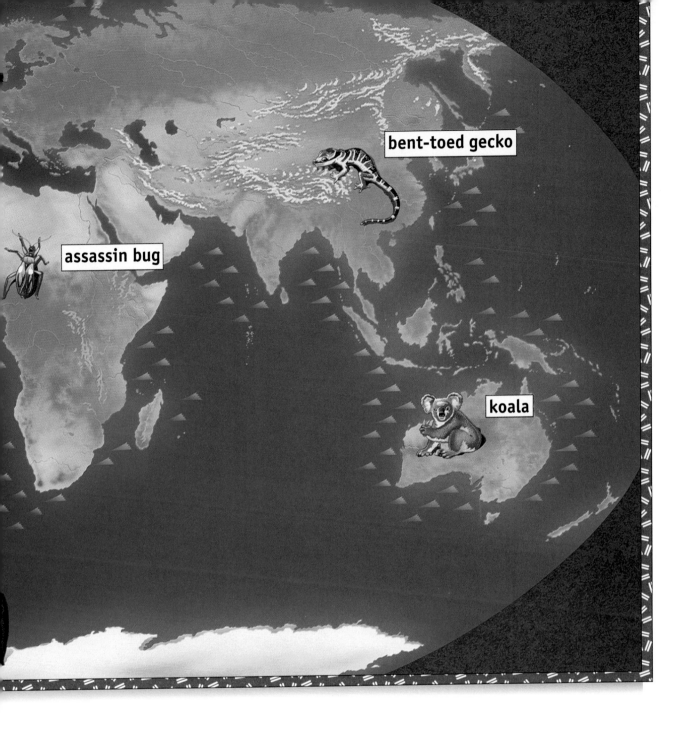

assassin bug

bent-toed gecko

koala

Different kinds of animals are shown. One animal is shown on each continent. Each place is different. Some places are hot. Other places are cold. Some places are wet. Other places are dry. That's why different animals and plants live in each place.

Examining
Plants

WHAT YOU NEED

variety of live plants

hand lens

Science Notebook

1. Look at the different plants. Use a hand lens to look at the different parts.

2. Look for, ways that the plants are all the same.

3. Record your findings.

Think! How are all these plants alike?

How Plants Are Alike

Plants are living things. Plants need water to grow. They also need light and air. Plants stay in one place unless moved.

Many plants have the same parts. Most plants have roots, stems, and leaves. Many have flowers.

Roots grow down in soil. **Roots** take in water. Most stems grow above ground. **Stems** carry water from the roots to other plant parts.

Leaves grow on a stem or up from the roots. Leaves make food for the plant. **Flowers** make seeds that grow into new plants.

Grouping Plots

WHAT YOU NEED

variety of live plants   hand lens   Science Notebook

1. Look at the different plants.
Talk about how each one looks.

2. Think of a way to group the plants.

3. Group the plants and record your groupings.

Think! What makes one plant different from another?

Comparing Plants

The same plant parts can be different. Look at the pictures. How are these plants different?

You see flowers on two plants. The spruce tree doesn't have flowers. It has cones. The picture of the apple tree shows fruit.

The trees grow very tall. The rosebush and sunflower don't grow as tall. The sunflower has big, flat leaves. The spruce tree has thin, pointed leaves. This kind of leaf is called a **needle**.

Think of some other plants. How are they different from these?

Examining Animals

WHAT YOU NEED
---

variety of live animals

Science Notebook

---

1. Look at the different animals.

2. Look for ways that the animals are all the same.

3. Record your findings.

Think! How are all animals alike?

How Animals Are Alike

Animals are living things. They are alike in
many ways. Many kinds of animals live in a
swamp. How are these animals alike? All
animals have a body covering. They all need
food. They all need water. All animals need air.

Animals can move. They move from place to place. They move to find food. They also move to get away from danger.

Animals need homes. They need homes for shelter. They need homes for safety. All kinds of animals can make baby animals.

Watching
Animals Move

══ WHAT YOU NEED ══

variety of live animals

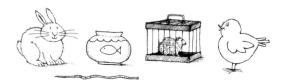

Science Notebook

1. Go to the front of the classroom. Record how your body moved and what body parts you used.

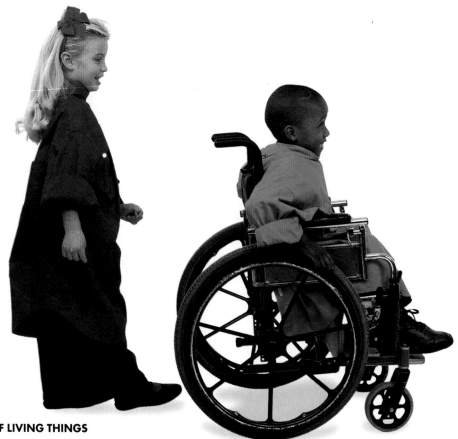

2. Observe each animal. Record how it moves.

3. Look at each animal's body parts. Record the body parts that each animal uses to move.

Think! How do body parts help an animal move?

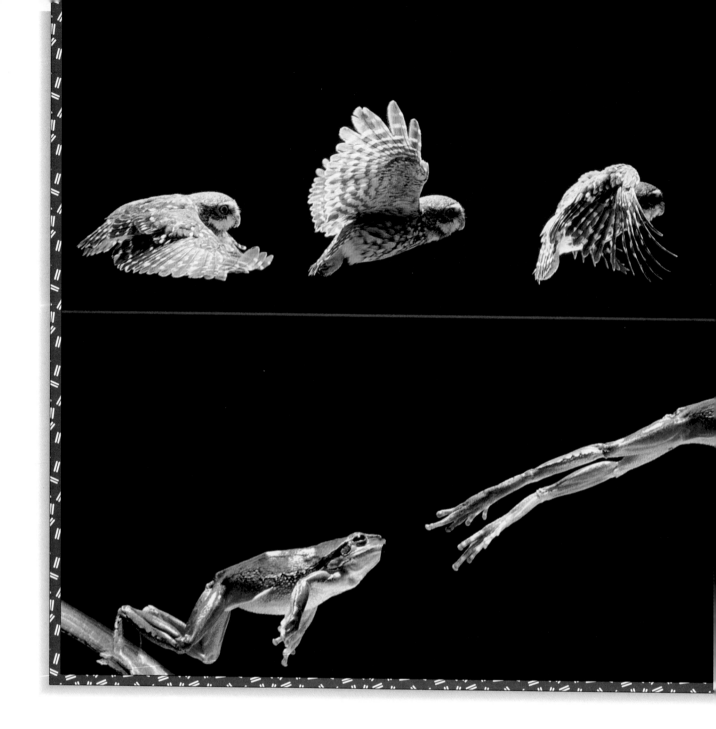

How Animals Move

All animals move. They move in different ways. How do these animals move?

The owl flies. The frog jumps. What other ways do animals move? Some animals crawl. Others swim. Some just walk or run.

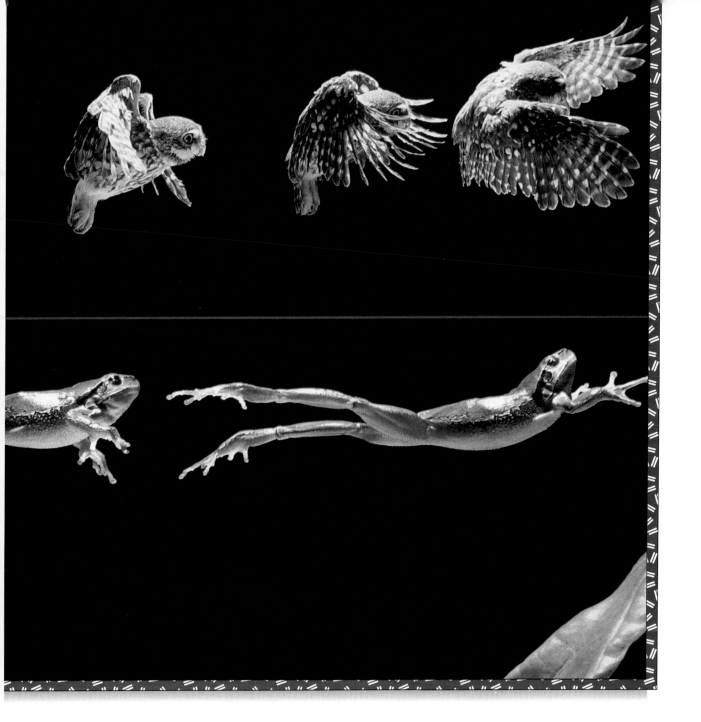

What body parts help animals move? An owl has wings. Wings are good for flying.

A frog has long back legs. Strong legs are good for jumping. Legs are also used for walking and running. Some animals have fins. Fins help an animal swim.

Examining
Body Coverings

WHAT YOU NEED

hand lens

feathers of different birds

dried fish scales

Science Notebook

1. Use a hand lens to look at your skin. Draw what you see.

2. Use the hand lens to look at feathers. Draw what you see.

3. Look at fish scales. Draw what you see.

4. Compare your drawings.

Think! How are skin, feathers, and fish scales alike and different?

Body Coverings

All animals have a body covering. Many are covered by **skin**. Some animals have a covering over their skin. Look at the many body coverings. Find hair. It can be long. It can be short. Thick **hair** is called fur.

Look for feathers. **Feathers** cover a bird's skin. Look for scales. **Scales** are thin and flat. Fish and snakes have scales. Now find a shell. Most shells are hard. Turtles have shells.

What animal belongs to each body covering? Turn the page to find out.

Body coverings help animals. Hair helps keep
a dog warm. Feathers help keep a bird warm
and dry. Skin can help keep animals cool.

Skin can also help keep an animal safe. Scales
help keep a fish from getting cut. A shell helps
keep a turtle safe.

Body coverings can also help animals move. Feathers help birds fly through the air. Scales help fish swim through the water.

Body coverings can be many colors. What colors do you see in the picture? Colors help you know each kind of animal.

Making a
Goldfish Home

WHAT YOU NEED

clear plastic container

container of water

assorted aquarium materials

Science Notebook

1. Plan a home you can make for a goldfish. Record your plan.

2. Make your goldfish home.

3. Predict what the goldfish will do when you put it in the home. Record your prediction.

4. Put a goldfish in the home. Record what the goldfish does.

Think! How does a goldfish use the things in its home for shelter and safety?

Some Animal Homes

All animals need homes. Some animals have homes in water. Some have homes in trees. Other animals make their homes underground. Some animals carry their homes with them. Other animals share homes.

A home gives an animal shelter. A **shelter** helps keep an animal safe. Look at the homes in the picture. Two of them are made in trees. How are these homes different?

What kinds of animals might live in each home? Turn the page to find out.

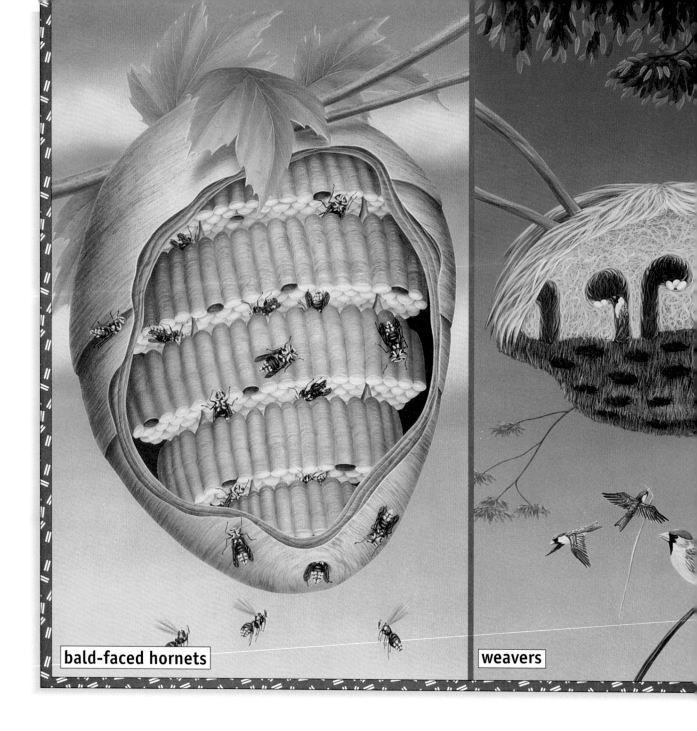

bald-faced hornets

weavers

These animals all live inside their homes. The hornets and birds build their homes. The bats don't build their home.

Some animals build homes for their babies. The bird's nest helps keep the baby birds safe. The cave also keeps baby bats safe.

KINDS OF LIVING THINGS

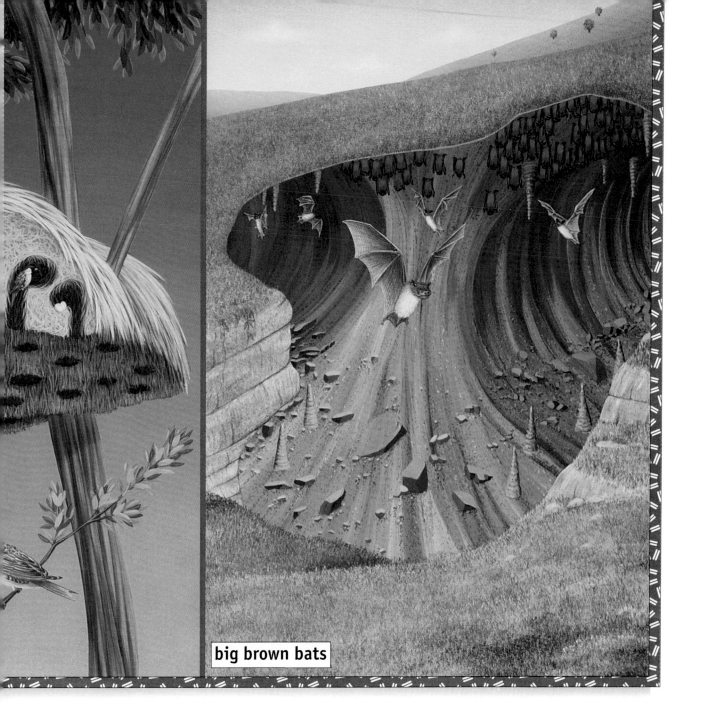

big brown bats

Some animals use their homes to store food. The hornets use their hive to store food. Squirrels store nuts in their tree homes.

Think about your home. It gives you shelter from the cold. It helps keep you safe. How is your home like other animal homes?

Looking at Teeth

carrot sticks

mirror

Science Notebook

1. Take a bite of a carrot stick. Record which teeth you used.

2. Use a mirror to look at those teeth. Record what they look like.

3. Chew the carrot stick. Record which teeth you used.

4. Use the mirror to look at those teeth. Record what they look like.

Think! How are teeth used for biting different than teeth used for chewing?

Comparing Teeth

All animals need food to live. Different animals eat different foods. Animals have mouth parts that help them eat. Look at the picture. How are the teeth different? The zebra has flat teeth. The lion has pointed teeth.

How does each animal's teeth help it eat? The zebra's flat teeth can grind plants. A zebra is a **plant eater**. The lion's pointed teeth can tear meat. Lions are **meat eaters**.

We have flat teeth. We also have pointed teeth. We can eat both plants and meat.

Grouping Animals

discarded magazines

scissors

Science Notebook

1. Cut out pictures of different kinds of animals.

2. Group the animals by their body covering.

3. Group the animals in a different way. Record your groups.

Think! How are the animals in one group alike?

basset hounds

walruses

spotted dolphins

African elephants

Many Kinds of Mammals

All of these animals are mammals. Mammals are one group of animals. How are they all alike? All **mammals** have hair. They feed milk to their babies. How are the mammals in the picture different?

white-tailed deer

crab-eating macaque

white-footed mice

gray kangaroos

Some mammals live in water. Others live on land. Some mammals swim. Some have tusks. Some mammals eat meat. Others eat plants.

Other kinds of animals make other groups. Animals with feathers are birds. What other animal groups can you think of?

Word Power

A. Match the words with a picture.

feathers   hair   scales

a.   **b.**   **c.**

B. Use these words to fill in the blanks.

needle   mammal   shelter

plant eater   meat eater

1. An animal that feeds milk to its babies is a _____.

2. An animal with pointed teeth is a _____.

3. A thin, pointed leaf is called a _____.

4. An animal with flat teeth is a _____.

5. A place where an animal goes to be safe is a _____.

Using Science Ideas

How could you group these plants?

Solving Science Problems

1. How are a goldfish and a guinea pig the same? How are they different?

2. Make a chart like the one shown. Add more animal names. Fill in the spaces.

Animal	Body Covering	How It Moves
bird	feathers	flies
wolf		
fish		

WEATHER AND SEASONS

Theme: Constancy and Change

Recording Weather Observations

WHAT YOU NEED

weather chart

crayons

weather symbols

scissors

glue

thermometer

wind profiler

Science Notebook

1. Look at the sky. Record whether it is sunny, cloudy, or foggy.

2. Measure and record the temperature.

3. Look for signs of wind blowing. Record how strong it is.

4. Look for precipitation. Record what you see.

5. Repeat steps 1–4 each day.

Think! How did the weather change?

Monday

Tue

Weather Changes

Is it sunny? Is it windy? Is it raining? These are questions about the air outside. These are questions about **weather**.

The weather changes each day. Look at the pictures. How did the weather change each day?

Wednesday

On Monday, it was sunny. On Tuesday, it was raining. On Wednesday, it was windy. What might the weather be on Thursday?

One way weather changes is that the air gets hotter or colder. The **temperature** of the air tells how hot or cold it is outside.

Exploring the Sun's Warmth

WHAT YOU NEED

2 chocolate kisses

2 sealable bags

2 thermometers

stopwatch

Science Notebook

1. Put a chocolate kiss into each plastic bag.

2. Place one bag and a thermometer in the sun. Record the temperature.

3. Repeat step 2 in the shade.

4. Record both temperatures after 10 minutes and after 20 minutes.

5. Look at the chocolate kisses in the bags. Record the changes you see.

Think! What do you think caused the changes in the chocolate?

The Warmth of the Sun

The sun heats our land. It heats our rivers and oceans, too. It even heats the air around us.

When the air is hot, we feel hot. When the air is cold, we feel cold. People, animals, and plants need sunlight.

Look at the picture. The children on the
swings are in sunlight. The air around them is
warm. They feel warm.

The children in the sandbox are in **shade**. A
tree blocks some of the sunlight. The air around
these children is cooler. They feel cooler.

Getting Warmer

WHAT YOU NEED

4 thermometers

stopwatch

Science Notebook

1. Place a thermometer in your shadow on the grass. Wait 2 minutes. Record the temperature.

2. Repeat step 1, placing the thermometer on asphalt.

3. Repeat step 1, placing the thermometer on concrete.

4. Repeat step 1, placing the thermometer on soil.

5. Compare the temperatures in different places.

**Think! Why were some places
warmer than other places?**

Warm or Hot?

It's a bright and sunny day! The sun shines on many things. It shines on the cement. It shines on the water. It shines on the people.

Some things get warm. Others get hot. These things take in the **heat** of the sun.

What things would feel hot? The cement
would feel hot. It takes in a lot of heat. The water
does not take in as much heat. It would not feel
as hot as the cement.

Dark colors take in more heat than light colors.
Would the boy's shirt or shorts feel hotter?

Exploring Wind

WHAT YOU NEED

pinwheel pattern

scissors

cellophane tape

push pin

pencil with an eraser

Science Notebook

1. Cut on the dotted lines of the pattern. Cut toward the square in the center.

2. Fold the corners with dots in toward the center and tape them in place.

3. Put a push pin through the center of the pinwheel and into the eraser of a pencil.

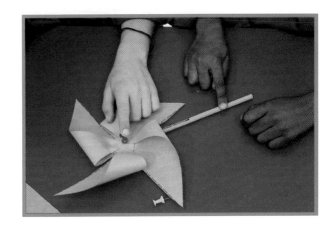

4. Try different ways to make your pinwheel turn. Record what you try and what happens.

Think! What made the pinwheel turn?

Blowing in the Wind

Weather changes. The wind also changes. Wind is moving air.

Sometimes the wind moves fast. Sometimes the wind moves slowly. Think of a time that you have seen the wind move something.

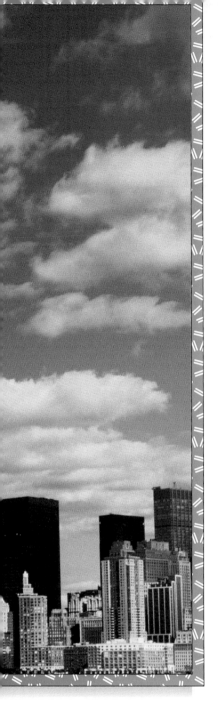

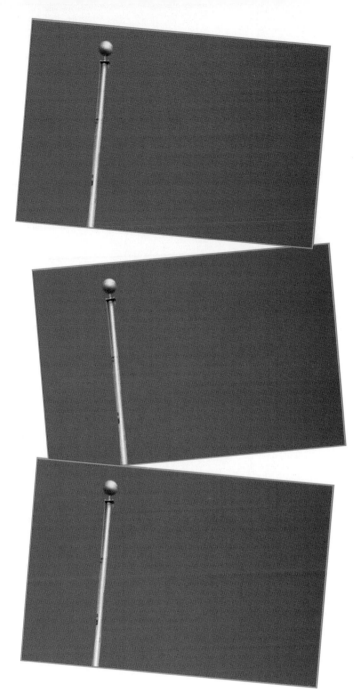

The wind blows hats off heads. It moves sailboats. It blows snow into drifts. It turns pinwheels. The wind also makes flags wave.

How would this flag look if there were no wind? How would it look if there were a lot of wind? Turn the page to find out.

In the top picture, there is no wind. The air is **calm**. The flag is not waving. Sailboats don't sail. Pinwheels don't turn.

In the middle picture, there is a little wind. The flag waves slowly when there's a **breeze**. Sailboats sail. Pinwheels turn.

In the bottom picture, there is a lot of wind. The flag waves quickly when there is a **strong wind**. Sailboats sail fast. Pinwheels turn fast.

When the winds are very strong, the air moves very quickly. Some of the strongest winds blow in a hurricane. This can cause a lot of damage.

Examining Condensation

WHAT YOU NEED

2 small cans

container of colored water

cup of ice cubes

stopwatch

Science Notebook

1. Feel the outside of an empty can. Record how it feels.

2. Put ice cubes into another can. Add water.

3. Wait 5 minutes. Feel the outside of the can of ice water. Record what you see and feel.

Think! How are the outsides of the two cans different?

Water in the Air

The water we drink is a liquid. Water can also be a solid. Ice is solid water. Water can also be a gas. Water as a gas is called **water vapor**.

Look at the picture. Where did the spot on the window come from?

There was water vapor in the girl's breath. Her breath was warm. The window was cold. When she breathed on the window, the water vapor changed to liquid water.

High in the sky, water vapor also changes to liquid water. Drops of liquid water form **clouds**.

Some people might say the girl is making the window foggy. Fog is a cloud close to the ground. Fog, clouds, and the spot on the window are all made of tiny drops of water.

In clouds, many tiny drops join to make bigger drops. When they get very big, they fall as rain.

If the drops of rain get colder, they can change to ice. This solid water can fall as snow, as hail, or as sleet.

Water vapor near the ground might cool. It can form tiny drops of water on objects. This water is called dew. If these drops freeze, they form frost.

Going on a
Scavenger Hunt

WHAT YOU NEED

scavenger hunt list paper bag Science Notebook

1. Go on a scavenger hunt. Collect as many items from the list as you can.

2. Talk about items that you collected and any items that you could not find.

3. Predict how the list might be different in another season.

4. Make up a scavenger hunt list to use during another season.

Think! How does the season affect the items you can find?

Looking at Seasons

The pictures show the same place in all four seasons. A **season** is a time of the year.

The four seasons are spring, summer, autumn, and winter. Weather changes from season to season. What changes do you see?

In **spring**, plants bloom and the air is warm. When **summer** comes, the air gets even warmer. Then in **autumn**, it gets cool. The leaves fall off the trees.

Finally, in **winter**, the air gets cold. The trees are bare. What are the seasons like where you live?

Cooling Off and Warming Up

crayons

Science Notebook

1. Brainstorm with your group ways to cool off on a hot day. Record your ideas.

2. Brainstorm with your group ways to warm up on a cold day. Record your ideas.

3. Take turns acting out your ideas. Have other groups try to guess how you cool off or warm up.

Think! How do people cool off and warm up?

Weather and Seasons
Cooling Off | Warming Up

People and Seasons

What fun it is to play outside! You can have fun in all four seasons.

Hot weather is shown in one picture. Cold weather is shown in the other picture. How can you tell what the weather is like in each picture?

WEATHER AND SEASONS

People wear less clothing when it is hot outside. It is hot in summer. Some people swim to cool their bodies when it's hot.

People wear more clothing when it is cold outside. It is cold in winter. People change what they do and wear as the seasons change.

Keeping Warm

WHAT YOU NEED

paper towel

ice cube in a sealable plastic bag

stopwatch

fiberfill

Science Notebook

1. Pretend you are an animal and the paper towel is your thin summer coat. Hold an ice cube on the paper towel for 1 minute. Record how it feels.

2. Pretend the fluffy stuff is your thick winter coat. Put it between the paper towel and your arm.

3. Hold the ice cube on top of your thick winter coat for 1 minute. Record how it feels.

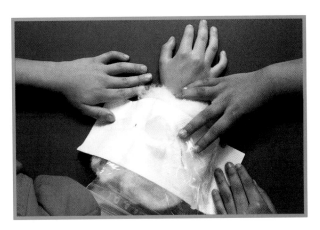

Think! How does a thick winter coat help an animal?

Animals and Seasons

Animals also change with the seasons. The first picture shows a weasel in summer.

The second picture shows a weasel in winter. It has white fur in winter. This color helps the weasel hide in the snow.

Some animals get ready for winter in other ways. Many grow thick fur coats that keep them warm. Birds fly to warm places. They **migrate**. Frogs sleep in the mud all winter. They **hibernate**. The insides of their bodies slow down, so they don't need much food.

Watching Seeds Grow

WHAT YOU NEED

2 parts of egg carton

soil

radish seeds

spray bottle with water

refrigerator

Science Notebook

1. Put soil in egg cartons. Plant a radish seed in each egg cup.

2. Water all seeds the same amount. Do not overwater.

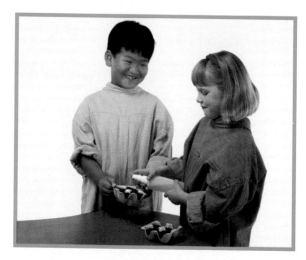

3. Put some seeds in a refrigerator. Put the other seeds in a warm place. Water the seeds every day.

4. Compare the two containers of seeds. Record what you see.

Think! How does temperature affect how seeds grow?

Plants and Seasons

Plants also change with the seasons. The pictures show an oak tree in each of the four seasons. The large picture is autumn. How can you tell? The leaves have changed color. What seasons are the other pictures?

The top picture is winter. It has gotten colder. The leaves have fallen from the tree. The next picture is spring. The air has gotten warmer. There are buds on the tree. The bottom picture is summer. There are many green leaves. What will the tree look like next?

Word Power

A. Match the words with a picture.

calm   breeze   strong wind

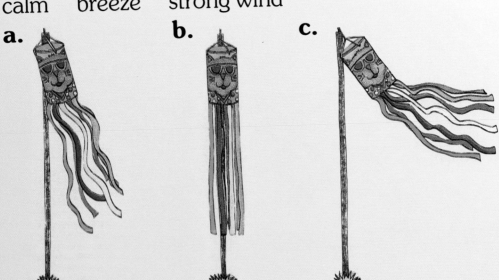

a.   **b.**   **c.**

B. Use these words to fill in the blanks.

temperature   migrate   water vapor
shade   hibernate

1. Birds _____ to warm places.

2. Frogs _____ in mud for the winter.

3. The _____ of the air is how hot or cold it is.

4. When you breathe on a window, _____ changes to liquid water.

5. When a tree blocks sunlight, there is _____ under the tree.

Using Science Ideas

What season is shown? How can you tell?

Solving Science Problems

1. Which feels warmer in the sun—cement or water? Why?

2. Make a chart like the one shown. Fill in what plants look like in each season. Then fill in what people wear or do in each season.

Season	Plants	People
spring		
summer		
autumn		
winter		

MAGNETS

Themes: Systems; Scale

Exploring
Magnetic Attraction

WHAT YOU NEED

bag of objects

magnet

Science Notebook

1. Predict whether a magnet will attract each object. Record your predictions.

2. Test the objects and record your results.

3. Compare your results with your predictions. Talk about which results surprised you.

Think! What did you find out about the objects that magnets attract?

Things Magnets Attract

A magnet is a piece of metal. It can pull some things toward itself and hold them. The magnet **attracts** these things. Look at the picture. Which things might a magnet attract? A **magnet** attracts things made of iron, steel, and nickel.

Magnets do not attract <u>all</u> things. A magnet will not pick up a paper. It will not pick up a plastic bag. It will not pick up most soda cans. These things are not made of iron, steel, or nickel. Look at the picture again. What other things will a magnet not attract?

Discovering
Magnetic Force

WHAT YOU NEED

2 pieces of tape

paper clip tied to a piece of yarn

magnet

objects to test

Science Notebook

1. Tape the ends of the yarn to a table.

2. Touch a magnet to a paper clip. Use the magnet to make the paper clip stand up.

3. Slowly pull the magnet up so it's not touching the paper clip.

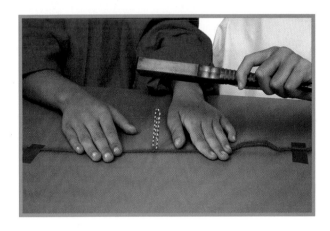

4. Put different objects between the clip and the magnet. Record what happens.

Think! Which objects made the clip fall? How are they alike?

Force of Magnets

A magnet can attract things without touching them. These trucks have paper clips on them. The magnets and the paper clips are not touching. The magnets attract the paper clips. The trucks move as the magnets move.

A magnet has a force around it. Magnetic force goes through the air. It also goes through some things.

Put a paper clip on one side of a paper. Then move a magnet on the other side. The paper clip moves. Magnetic force goes through paper.

Comparing
Parts of a Magnet

WHAT YOU NEED

bar magnet

paper clip

Science Notebook

1. Hold up a bar magnet and make a paper-clip chain at one end. Count the paper clips and record the number.

2. Remove the clips. Make a new chain in the middle of the magnet. Count the clips and record the number.

3. Remove the clips and make a chain at the other end of the magnet. Count the clips and record the number.

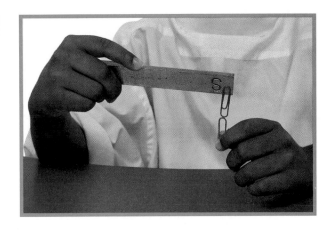

4. Make a bar graph to show the number of clips in each chain. Compare the numbers.

Think! What does your bar graph tell you about the parts of your bar magnet?

Strength of Magnets

Some magnets are stronger than others.

Some strong magnets can pick up a car.

Look at the picture. Which magnet is the largest? The **bar magnet** is one of the largest. It is the long, straight silver magnet.

Point to the smaller magnets. Which magnet can pick up the most paper clips?

You might think the bar magnet can pick up the most clips. You might think a small magnet can pick up just a few clips. Turn the page to find out which magnet is strongest.

Each magnet picked up some clips. The picture helps you compare the strength of the magnets. A small magnet can be strong. A large magnet can be weak. The bar magnet picked up just six paper clips. Some of the smaller magnets picked up many paper clips.

Look again at the bar magnet. The clips are
hanging from each end. The ends of the magnet
are called **poles**. Magnetic force is strongest at a
magnet's poles. How can you find the poles of
the other magnets? The poles are where the
clips are hanging.

Observing the
Poles of Magnets

WHAT YOU NEED

5 bar magnets

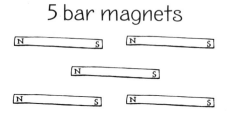

Science Notebook

1. Place two magnets end to end and record what happens.

2. Turn one of the magnets around and record what happens.

3. Place five magnets end to end so that they stick together. Draw the line of magnets and label the poles.

Think! What did you learn about pushes and pulls at the ends of the magnets?

Attract or Repel?

Bar magnets are on these toys. Look at one magnet. The N shows the north pole. The S shows the south pole.

Look at the train. North poles are next to south poles. Unlike poles always attract each other.

Look at the boats. North poles are next to north poles. South poles are next to south poles. Like poles push away from each other. Like poles always **repel**. How can you get the boats to connect? Turn some boats so that unlike poles are next to each other.

Making Magnetic Patterns

WHAT YOU NEED

goggles

2 bar magnets

3 sheets of white paper

jar of iron filings with shaker lid

Science Notebook

1. Place a sheet of paper on top of one magnet. Sprinkle iron filings onto the paper. Draw what you see.

2. Lay two magnets end to end, but not touching. Cover them with paper.

3. Slowly sprinkle iron filings onto the paper. Draw what you see.

4. Turn one magnet around. Cover both magnets with paper. Sprinkle iron filings onto the paper. Draw what you see.

Think! How are your three drawings alike? How are they different?

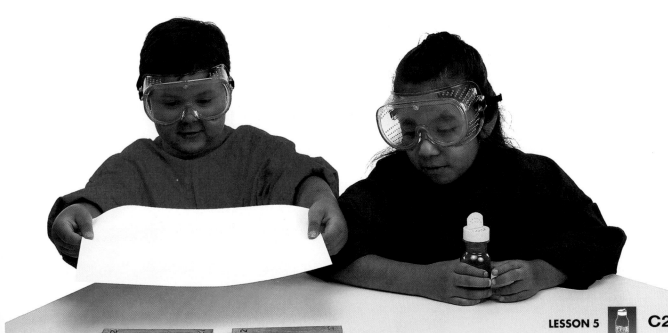

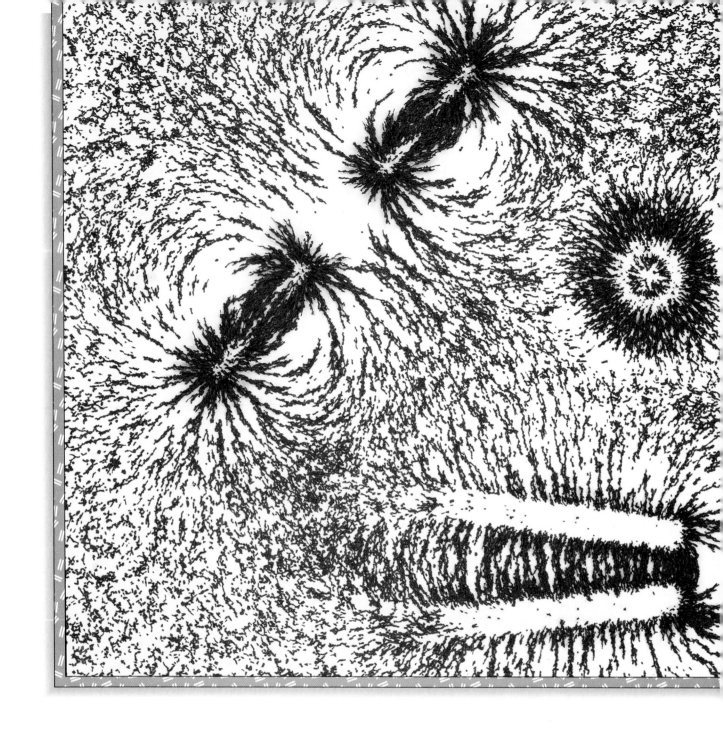

What's Around a Magnet?

Each magnet can make its own pattern. Look at the patterns. They are made of iron filings.

The patterns show the magnetic field of each magnet. A **magnetic field** is all around a magnet. It's where a magnet's force is felt.

Look for places where there are the most iron filings. That's where the force is strong.

Now look for places where there are few iron filings. That's where the force is weak. What magnets made these patterns? Turn the page to find out.

Think about the picture you just saw. It was made with these magnets.

A sheet of paper was put on top of the magnets. Iron filings were sprinkled on the paper. The filings made patterns. The patterns show the magnetic fields.

Look at one of the red magnets. The letters N and S are on the poles. Now look back at the picture of iron filings. You see a lot of iron filings between the two poles. This shows the attraction between two unlike poles. Which two bar magnets have unlike poles?

Making Magnets

WHAT YOU NEED

goggles

metal spoon

jar of iron filings

magnet

Science Notebook

1. Dip a spoon into some iron filings. Remove the spoon and draw what you see.

2. Use a magnet to stroke the spoon ten times in one direction.

3. Dip the spoon into the iron filings again. Remove it and draw what you see.

Think! Compare your drawings. What happened to the spoon?

Making a Magnet

Look at the picture story. The girl wants to fish, too. She makes a magnet. A **temporary magnet** won't last long. The girl uses a steel key. She strokes it with the boy's magnet. She strokes it many times in the same way.

MAGNETS

Think of things that a magnet attracts. You can use any of those things to make a temporary magnet. What can you use?

You can use an iron nail. You can also use a steel spoon. A plastic jar isn't made of iron or steel. You can't use it to make a magnet.

Using a
Magnet as a Compass

pan of water

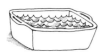

plate

bar magnet

compass

Science Notebook

1. Float a plate in a pan of water.

2. Put a magnet in the center of the plate. Record what happens.

3. Compare the poles of the magnet with the needle on a compass. Record what you see.

Think! How are the magnet and the compass alike?

Finding Your Way

The earth is like a bar magnet. It has a north pole. It also has a south pole.

A compass needle is a bar magnet. It has a north-seeking pole. This pole points the same way as the earth's north pole.

The people in these photos are using compasses. A **compass** is a tool. It is used to show direction.

The hikers turn the compass. They turn it until the needle points to the N. This tells them which way is north. Then they know which way to go.

Word Power

A. Match the words with a picture.

bar magnet   compass   temporary magnet

a.    **b.**    **c.**

B. Use these words to fill in the blanks.

attract   magnet   repel
poles   magnetic field

1. The space around a magnet where the force is felt is the _____.

2. A _____ attracts things made of iron, steel, and nickel.

3. A magnet is strongest at its _____.

4. The north pole of one magnet will pull toward, or _____, the south pole of another magnet.

5. The north poles of two magnets push away, or _____, each other.

Using Science Ideas

a. Which things shown will a magnet attract? List or draw them.

b. Which things shown will a magnet not attract? List or draw them.

Solving Science Problems

1. How can you prove that magnets work through some things?

2. How can magnets help you?

UNIT D

EARTH'S LAND AND WATER

Themes: Systems; Models

Examining
Kinds of Soil

WHAT YOU NEED

goggles

topsoil

clay soil

sandy soil

hand lens

Science Notebook

1. Look at and touch each kind of soil.

2. Look at each kind of soil with a hand lens.

3. Record what you see.

Think! How are these kinds of soil alike, and how are they different?

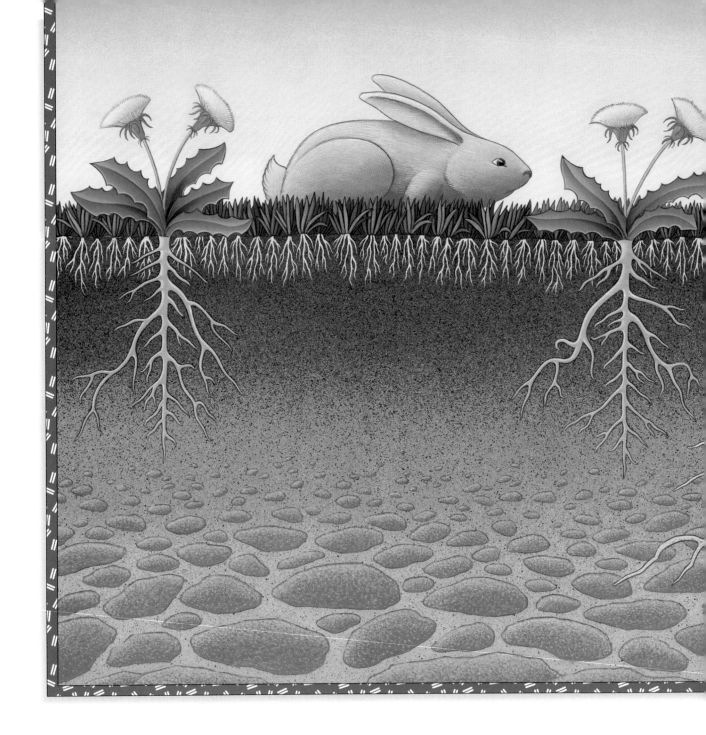

Looking at Soil

Soil covers much of the land. Look at the layers of soil in the picture. What's on the top layer? You see grass, a tree, and flowers. That's what you see when you look at the ground. You don't see the other layers.

The top part of soil is called **topsoil**. Roots grow down in the topsoil. The tree has the biggest roots. The grass has the smallest roots.

Clay soil is under the topsoil. Big rocks are under the clay soil. The tree's roots grow down to the rocks.

Analyzing
Soil

WHAT YOU NEED

goggles

2 large sheets of paper

cup of soil

hand lens

Science Notebook

1. Spread the soil out on a sheet of paper.

2. Use a hand lens to look at the soil.

3. Find things in the soil that are alike. Group these things on another sheet of paper.

4. Draw each group.

Think! **What kinds of objects did you find in the soil?**

Looking Closer at Soil

Soil is made of many things. The things in the picture can become part of soil. The logs and the leaves in the picture are **once-living things**. They are not living now. When they were living, they were part of a tree.

A tree is a living thing. **Living things** need air, water, and food to stay alive.

A rock is a nonliving thing. **Nonliving things** do not need air, water, and food. What kinds of things might you find under the log? Turn the page to find out.

The log has been rolled away. What living things do you see? You see bugs that live in soil. The hand lens makes them look a lot bigger than they are.

What nonliving things do you see? You see pieces of rock.

Look through the hand lens again. What once-living things do you see? You see pieces of dry leaves and twigs that were once part of a tree. They no longer need air, water, and food.

Think about a time that you looked under a rock or log. What kinds of things did you find?

Examining
Soil and Water

═══ WHAT YOU NEED ═══

goggles

paper towels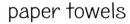

2 paper cups

moist soil

dry soil

spray bottle with water

Science Notebook

1. Place paper towels under cups. Fill half of one paper cup with moist soil. Fill half of another paper cup with dry soil.

2. Spray each cup 20 times with water. Count to 10.

3. Repeat step 2.

4. Record what happens.

Think! What happened to the water in each cup?

Water in Soil

Soil is made of tiny rocks and once-living things. There are many little spaces in soil. When it rains, water soaks into these spaces. When there is more water than the spaces in the soil can hold, puddles may form.

EARTH'S LAND AND WATER

Over time, some of the water from the puddles goes into the air. Water from the puddles may also slowly soak into the soil. The water in the soil is used by living things.

Look at the pictures. What living things use water in the soil?

Looking at Rocks

WHAT YOU NEED

goggles

rock samples

paper plates

Science Notebook

1. Spread out the rocks on a table.

2. Look at and feel each rock.

3. Group the rocks on paper plates.

4. Draw each group.

Think! How did you group the rocks?

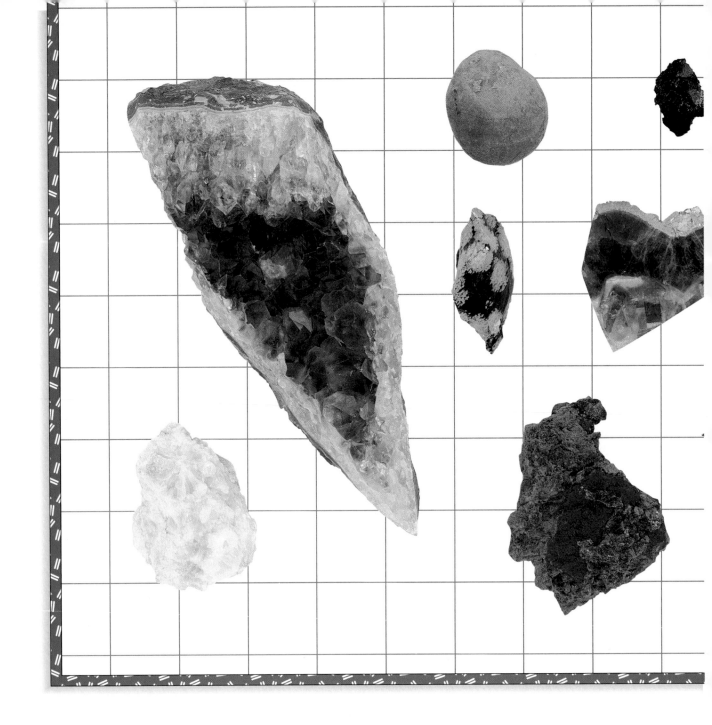

Grouping Rocks

Rocks come in many colors, shapes, and sizes.
Look at the rocks in the picture. What color
groups could you make? How would you group
the rocks by shape? Which rocks would you
group together by size?

Rocks can be grouped by the way they feel. Some rocks are smooth. Other rocks are not smooth. They are rough.

The white rock in the picture is rough. What other rocks might you put in a group of rough rocks? Which rocks are smooth?

Testing
Hardness of Rocks

WHAT YOU NEED

goggles

rocks

tile

Science Notebook

1. Spread rocks on a table.

2. Squeeze each rock in your hand. Record how each rock feels.

3. Now scratch each rock with your fingernail. Record what you observe.

4. Then scratch a tile with each rock. Record what you observe.

5. Compare the rocks.

Think! Which rocks were the hardest? Tell how you know.

sandstone

Looking at Hardness

Some rocks are harder than others. Hard rocks can **scratch**, or make a mark on, softer rocks. Soft rocks can't scratch harder rocks.

The pictures show two kinds of rocks. How can you tell which rock is harder?

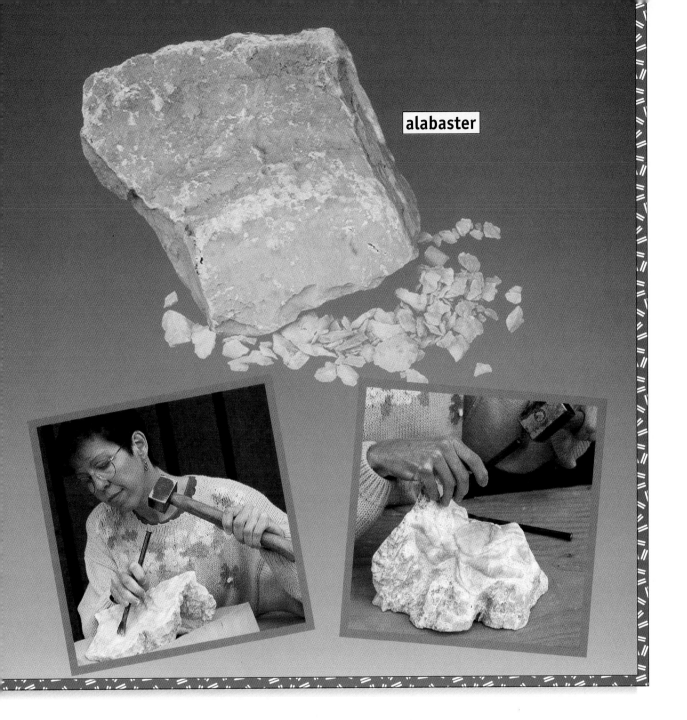

alabaster

The first artist is making powder from rock. The rock is soft. The artist uses the rock powder to make a picture.

The next artist is using harder rock. She uses a hammer to chip the rock. She chips away the rock to make a shape she likes.

Examining
Sizes of Rocks

WHAT YOU NEED

goggles   rock samples   sand

hand lens   Science Notebook

1. Spread rocks and sand on a table.

2. Look at each rock with a hand lens. Draw what you see.

3. Look at the sand with a hand lens. Draw what you see.

Think! How are the rocks and sand alike, and how are they different?

Looking at Size

Rocks come in many sizes. Very big rocks are called **boulders**.

The picture shows rocks of different sizes. The very big rock in the front is a boulder. It is the biggest rock in the picture.

EARTH'S LAND AND WATER

The rocks in the water are smaller than the boulder. After a long time, the water will wear away the rocks. The water will make the rocks smaller. What might you find on the bottom of the river? You might find small rocks and sand. **Sand** is made up of tiny pieces of rock.

Observing
How Water Flows

WHAT YOU NEED

goggles

wet sand

pan

button

measuring cup with water

Science Notebook

1. Use wet sand to make a small hill in a pan.

2. Put a button in a place where you predict water will flow.

3. Slowly pour one cup of water from the measuring cup onto the top of the hill.

4. Watch where the water flows. Record what you see.

Think! Where did the water flow?

Moving Water

Water always goes downhill. Sometimes it goes fast. Sometimes it goes slowly.

The pictures show water going downhill. In the first picture, the water goes fast at the top. At the bottom, the water goes slowly.

The other pictures also show water going fast. What shows that the water is going fast?

Moving water can cut a path in the ground. A small path of moving water is called a **stream**. When a stream gets bigger, it is a **river**. You see a river in the first picture.

Observing
How Water Gathers

WHAT YOU NEED

goggles

large plastic dishpan

soil

3 measuring cups of water

Science Notebook

1. Cover the bottom of a dishpan with soil. Use your hands to push down the soil in the middle of the pan.

2. Pour 3 cups of water into the dishpan.

3. Watch where the water flows.

4. Record what you see.

Think! What happened to the water?

Puddles and Lakes

Water that doesn't soak into the ground forms
a puddle. It can dry up in the sunshine.

Water from springs and rivers can form a lake.
A **lake** has a lot of water in it. A lake does not
dry up in the sunshine.

Look at the picture. Where is the water
flowing? It is flowing downhill and into a lake.

You can see a boat and a swimming area on
the lake. Lakes and rivers need to be kept clean.
Then we can have fun there. How might you
help keep a lake or river clean?

Making Compost

WHAT YOU NEED

goggles

2 small milk cartons

soil

spoon

banana peel

plastic cap

spray bottle with water

Science Notebook

1. Fill each carton with soil.

2. Bury a banana peel in carton 1 and a cap in carton 2. Put both cartons in a warm place.

3. Spray each carton 10 times and then close each carton.

4. Repeat step 3 each day for four weeks.

5. Uncover the objects once a week and record what you see.

Think! How did the objects change?

Making Compost

Recycling means using things again. This woman is making compost. **Compost** is something made by recycling once-living things.

Look at the large photo. The woman is adding food scraps to the pile.

Look at the small photos. The woman mixes leaves and grass clippings with the scraps. Then she stirs the pile. In time, these things will break down to become compost.

The woman adds the compost to the soil around her plants to help them grow.

Word Power

A. Match the words with a picture.

stream   river   lake

a.

b.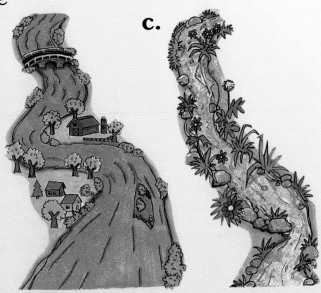

c.

B. Use these words to fill in the blanks.

recycle   sand   compost
scratch   boulder

1. Hard rocks can _____ softer rocks.

2. A very big rock is called a _____.

3. When you use things again, you _____.

4. Many small bits of rock are called _____.

5. You can recycle food scraps into _____ and add it to the soil around plants.

Using Science Ideas

a. List the once-living things you see in the picture.

b. List the nonliving things you see in the picture.

Solving Science Problems

1. What layers of soil do tree roots grow through?

2. Explain how you can recycle food scraps.

UNIT E

KEEPING FIT AND HEALTHY

Themes: Systems; Constancy and Change

Grouping Foods

WHAT YOU NEED

empty food containers

6 grocery bags with labels

Science Notebook

1. Bring in empty food containers from home.

2. Sort the containers into food groups.

3. Draw a picture of the food in each group. Name each food.

4. Think of other foods to add to these groups. Tell why you think they belong.

Think! What kinds of foods should you eat the most? Tell how you decided.

The Food Pyramid

The picture shows a food pyramid. It tells about the foods you need each day to stay healthy. There are six food groups in the food pyramid. A **food group** has like kinds of food. Milk, yogurt, and cheese are one food group.

The biggest food group is bread, cereal, rice, and pasta. Your body needs a lot of these foods.

The smallest food group is fats, oils, and sweets. You only need a little food from this group. Candy and butter are in this group. What are the other food groups?

The **food pyramid** tells how many servings of food your body needs. A roll is one **serving** of bread. An apple is one serving of fruit.

You should eat two to four servings of fruit each day. How many servings of milk, yogurt, and cheese does your body need?

KEEPING FIT AND HEALTHY

Your body needs many kinds of foods to stay healthy. You should choose food from each food group every day.

What is your favorite food? Where is it on the food pyramid? How many servings do you need from that group each day?

Fishing for a Balanced Meal

food pictures

scissors

glue

paper fish

paper clips

paper fish pond

magnet on a string

Science Notebook

1. Cut out pictures of food. Glue each picture to a paper fish.

2. Put a paper clip on each fish. Put your fish in a paper pond.

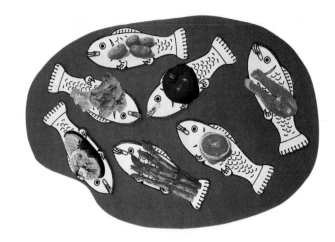

3. Fish for a balanced meal.

4. Glue the meal onto your plate.

Think! What makes a meal balanced?

Combining Foods

Many people eat three meals a day. They eat breakfast early in the day. They eat lunch in the middle of the day. They eat dinner late in the day.

A **balanced meal** has food from many food groups. It has few fats or sweets.

KEEPING FIT AND HEALTHY

The pictures show balanced meals. The first meal has food from three food groups.

The cereal is from one group. The milk is from another group. The fruit is from a third group. Eating three balanced meals each day can help you stay healthy.

Testing
Snack Foods

WHAT YOU NEED

brown paper squares

bottle of cooking oil

snacks

Science Notebook

1. Write **oil** on one paper square. Put a drop of oil on that square.

2. Write the name of each food on a paper square. Rub each square with the food it names.

3. Hold each square up to the light. Compare each square to the square with oil. Record what you see.

Think! Which snacks are more healthful than others? Tell why you think so.

Good Snacks

Food you eat between meals is a **snack**. Some snacks are good for your body. Some are not.

There are snacks that have a lot of fat and oil in them. Potato chips and doughnuts have fat and oil in them.

The picture shows many foods. These foods make healthful snacks. Fruits are good snacks. Vegetables are good snacks. Snacks can be from more than one food group, too.

Pretend you are making a healthful snack. What would you put on the plate?

Exercising
Our Muscles

WHAT YOU NEED

6 exercise cards

Science Notebook

1. Choose an exercise card. Show the card to your group.

2. Do the exercise with your group.

3. Talk about which muscle you used the most. Record your ideas.

4. Repeat steps 1–3 using the other exercise cards.

Think! How do your muscles feel after you exercise them?

Moving Muscles

You have bones in your body. You have muscles in your body. **Muscles** help you move.

Look at the pictures. The children are playing. As they move, the children **exercise** their muscles.

KEEPING FIT AND HEALTHY

Look at the first picture. The boy is jumping rope. He is using the muscles in his arms and legs. What are the other children doing? What muscles are they using?

Exercise makes muscles and bones stronger. Exercise helps your body stay healthy.

Measuring Muscles

WHAT YOU NEED

2 construction paper strips

scissors

glue

Science Notebook

1. Put your arms at your sides. Have your partners measure around your upper arm with a paper strip. Mark the length.

2. Cut the paper strip at the mark. Glue the paper strip on a chart.

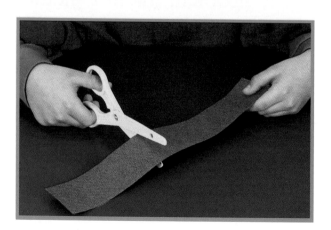

☺ **KEEPING FIT AND HEALTHY**

3. Make a muscle. Have your partners measure your arm again with another paper strip. Mark the length.

4. Cut the paper strip at the mark. Glue the paper strip on the chart. Compare the strips. Record your findings.

Think! How did the size of your arm muscle change?

Muscles and Bones

Look at the pictures. The children are making funny faces. They are moving their muscles to make the faces.

Muscles and bones work together. Muscles pull on bones to make the bones move.

Muscles in your face can help show how you feel. Make a face that shows you are happy. Feel the muscles and bones that make your face move.

Now make a face that shows you are sad. Feel the muscles. Compare the way your muscles moved each time.

Recording
My Sleep

WHAT YOU NEED

Science Notebook

1. Find out how many hours you slept last night.

2. Color a box on the graph for every hour you slept.

3. Repeat steps 1 and 2 for each night.

4. Record how you felt before going to sleep and after waking up.

**Think! How much sleep do you need?
Tell why you think so.**

Rest and Sleep

Look at the pictures. Follow the boy through his busy day. First, the boy walks to school. He is getting exercise.

Next, the boy does some work at school. Then he plays outside. After that, he rests a little.

You **rest** by sitting or lying down quietly. What things does the boy do after he rests?

Look at the last picture. The boy is sleeping. You give your body rest when you **sleep** at night. Your body needs rest and sleep to help it stay healthy. How do you rest each day?

Observing
Clean and Dirty Hands

WHAT YOU NEED

2 wet wipes

soap and water

Science Notebook

1. Predict whether your hands are clean or dirty. Record your prediction.

2. Wipe your hands with a wet wipe. Record what you find out.

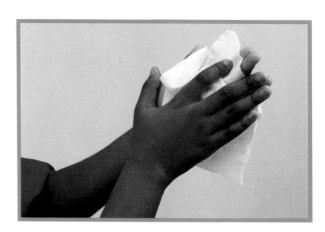

3. Wash your hands very carefully with soap and warm water.

4. Wipe your hands again with another wet wipe. Record what you find out.

Think! Why is washing your hands with soap and warm water important?

Good Health Habits

Germs can make you sick. They are very small. You can't see germs. But they are all around.

Good health habits help you stay well. You can wash with soap to kill germs. You can use a tissue to keep germs from spreading.

Look at the picture. Find people who are showing good health habits. Can you find the boy who is using a tissue when he sneezes? Do you see someone taking a bath?

Now find people who are not showing good health habits. What are they doing?

Brushing Out Stains

2 tiles

bottle of grape juice

toothbrush

toothpaste

Science Notebook

1. Put grape juice on two tiles. Let the tiles dry.

2. Use a toothbrush to brush tile 1. Record what happens.

3. Put toothpaste on the brush.

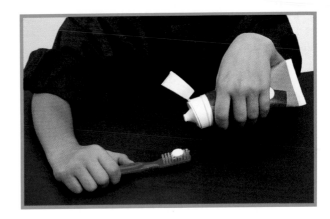

4. Brush tile 2. Record what happens.

Think! Which tile was easier to clean? Tell why you think so.

Caring for Teeth

Cleaning your teeth keeps them strong and healthy. Eating balanced meals also helps keep your teeth strong and healthy.

Look at the picture. The girl wants strong and healthy teeth. What things will help her?

She can eat an apple. It is a healthful food.
She can **brush** her teeth with a toothbrush and
toothpaste. She can use thin string called **floss**
to clean between her teeth.

What things are not good for her teeth? Candy
and other sweets are not good for teeth.

UNIT REVIEW

Word Power

A. Match the words with a picture.

food pyramid   exercise   balanced meal

a.

b.

c.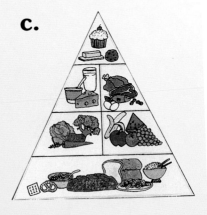

B. Use these words to fill in the blanks.

snack   brush   muscles
food groups   good health habit

1. You need to _____ your teeth to keep them clean.

2. Food you eat between meals is a _____.

3. There are six _____ in a food pyramid.

4. Washing your hands before you eat is a _____.

5. Your _____ help you move.

Using Science Ideas

What should these men do next?

Solving Science Problems

1. Why might you get sick if you eat only potato chips?

2. How does washing dishes help you keep fit and healthy?

SCIENCE Handbook

A scientist studies nature. A scientist thinks about ideas in a careful way. You can think like a scientist.

Observe

To think like a scientist, observe the things around you. Everything you hear and see is a clue about how the world works.

Two friends, Lisa and Carl, are spinning tops. They spin their tops at the same time. Each time, Carl's top is first to stop spinning.

Ask a Question

As you observe, you may see that some things happen over and over.
Ask questions about such things.

Lisa spins her top on a smooth floor.
Carl spins his on a rug. Lisa wonders,
does the kind of floor make Carl's top
stop first?

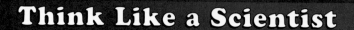

Make a Guess

Suppose you have an idea about why something happens. You make a guess based on your idea.

Lisa has an idea about what made Carl's top stop first. She thinks it might be the bumpy rug.

Plan and Do a Test

After you make a guess, plan how to test it. Then carry out your plan.

Lisa and Carl test the idea. Carl spins his top on the smooth table. Lisa spins her top on the bumpy cement.

Write What Happens

You need to observe your test carefully. Then write down what happens.

Lisa sees that her top slows down and stops sooner. She writes down what happened.

Draw Conclusions

Think about different reasons why something happened as it did.

Lisa thinks about the test.
She decides that bumps cause a
top to stop sooner.

Safety Tips

Wear your goggles when your teacher tells you.

Handle materials carefully.

Never put things into your mouth.

Wash your hands after every activity.

Be kind to living things.

Always tell an adult
if you are hurt.

Clean up spills.

Using a
Hand Lens

A hand lens is a tool that makes objects look bigger. It helps you see the small parts of an object.

Look at a Coin

1. Place a coin on your desk.

2. Hold the hand lens above the coin. Look through the lens. Slowly move the lens away from the coin. What do you see?

3. Keep moving the lens away until the coin looks blurry.

4. Then slowly move the lens closer. Stop when the coin does not look blurry.

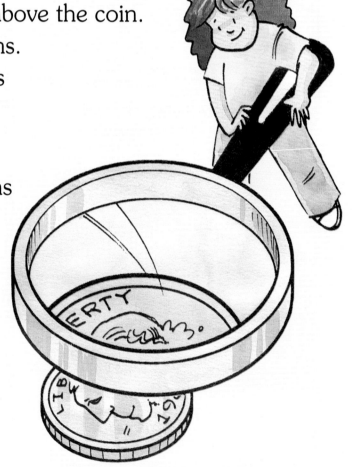

Using a
Thermometer

A thermometer is a tool used to measure temperature. Temperature tells how hot or cold something is. It is measured in degrees.

Find the Temperature of Water

1. Put water into a cup.

2. Put a thermometer into the cup.

3. Watch the colored liquid in the thermometer. What do you see?

4. Look how high the colored liquid is. What number is closest? That is the temperature of the water.

Using a Ruler

A ruler is a tool used to measure the length of objects. Most rulers are 12 inches long. This length is called a foot.

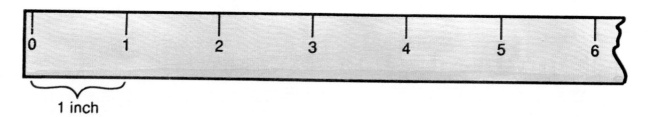

1 inch

Measure a Pencil

1. Place the ruler on your desk.

2. Lay your pencil next to the ruler. Line up one end with the 0 mark on the ruler.

3. Look at the other end of the pencil. Which number is closest to that end?

Using a Calculator

A calculator is a tool that can help you add numbers. It can help you subtract numbers.

Subtract Numbers

1. Tim and Anna both grew plants.
Tim grew 8 plants.
Anna grew 17 plants.

2. How many more plants did Anna grow?
Use your calculator to find out.

3. Enter 17 on the calculator.
Then press the ▬ key.
Enter 8 and press ▬ .

4. What is your answer?

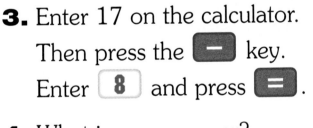

GLOSSARY

A

animals Animals are living things. They can move from place to place. Animals have body coverings. They eat other animals or plants for food. (A16)

attract Attract means to pull toward itself. A magnet attracts things made of iron, steel, and nickel. (C4)

autumn Autumn is the season of the year that comes before winter. Leaves fall off many trees in autumn. (B29)

B

balanced meal A balanced meal includes foods from most of the food groups on the food pyramid. (E10)

bar magnet A bar magnet is a long, straight piece of steel that has been magnetized. A bar magnet attracts things made of iron, steel, and nickel. (C12)

boulder A boulder is a very large rock. (D26)

breeze A breeze is a gentle wind. The breeze makes a flag wave slowly. (B18)

brush To brush means to clean one's teeth. When you brush your teeth, you remove food bits from them. (E35)

calm When the wind is calm, no wind is blowing. (B18)

clay soil Clay soil has a lot of clay in it. Clay soil is found below topsoil. (D5)

cloud A group of tiny drops of water in the air. Rain falls from some clouds. (B23)

compass A tool that is used to show direction. The needle of a compass always points north. (C32)

compost Compost is made by recycling once-living things. It can be added to soil to help plants grow. (D38)

exercise Exercise is moving your body. Playing outdoors is good exercise. (E18)

feathers Feathers cover the bodies of birds. Feathers keep birds warm. (A25)

flower A flower is a part of some plants. Seeds form in a flower. (A9)

floss Floss is thin string. It is used to clean between your teeth. Flossing removes food your toothbrush cannot reach. (E35)

food group A food group is made up of like kinds of food. Apples, bananas, grapes, and oranges are all part of the fruits group. (E4)

food pyramid The food pyramid shows the different food groups. It also shows how many servings of each group you should eat each day. (E6)

G

good health habits
Good health habits help you stay well. Washing your hands before you eat is a good health habit. (E30)

H

hair Hair covers the bodies of mammals. Hair helps mammals stay warm and protects their skin. (A24)

heat Heat is one kind of energy. The heat from the sun warms the earth. (B12)

hibernate When something hibernates, it sleeps through the winter. Many bears hibernate. (B37)

L

lake A lake is a body of water with land all around it. Water flows into lakes from rivers. (D34)

leaves Leaves are parts of plants. They make food for the plants. Leaves grow on stems or up from the roots. (A9)

living thing A living thing is alive. Living things need air, water, and food to grow. (D9)

magnet A magnet is a piece of metal. A magnet can attract things made of iron, steel, and nickel. (C4)

magnetic field The magnetic field is the area around a magnet. It is where the force of the magnet works. (C22)

mammal A mammal is one kind of animal. Mammals are covered with hair. They feed milk to their babies. (A40)

meat eater A meat eater is an animal that eats other animals. Meat eaters have sharp teeth to tear their food into pieces. (A37)

migrate When an animal migrates, it moves from place to place as the seasons change. Some birds migrate south for the winter. (B37)

muscles Muscles are body parts that help you move. The muscles in your legs help you run and jump. (E18)

needles Needles are thin and pointed leaves. The shape of needles helps keep water in the plant. (A13)

nonliving thing A nonliving thing was never alive. A rock is a nonliving thing. (D9)

once-living thing A once-living thing was alive at one time or was once part of a living thing. A feather and an acorn are once-living things. (D8)

plants Plants are living things. They need water, light, and air to grow. Most plants have roots, stems, and leaves. Many have flowers. (A8)

plant eater A plant eater is an animal that eats plants. A plant eater has flat teeth for grinding food. (A37)

poles Poles are the places on a magnet where the magnetic force is strongest. On a bar magnet, the poles are at the ends of the magnet. (C15)

R

recycling Recycling means using something again. Compost is made by recycling once-living things. (D38)

repel Repel means to push away or force apart. Like poles of two magnets repel each other. (C19)

rest When you rest, you lie down or sit quietly. After you exercise, you should rest. (E27)

river A river is a body of water. It flows in a long path. Rivers flow downhill into lakes and oceans. (D31)

root A root is a plant part. Roots grow down into the soil. Roots take in water from the soil. (A9)

S

sand Sand is made of very small rocks. Some ocean beaches are covered with sand. (D27)

scales Scales cover the bodies of fish and reptiles. Scales are thin and flat. (A25)

scratch When you scratch something, you make a mark on it. A harder rock will scratch a softer rock. (D22)

season A season is a time of the year. Spring, summer, autumn, and winter are the four seasons. (B28)

serving A serving is the right amount of a food that you should eat. A serving of cereal may be 1 cup. (E6)

shade An area that is out of the sun. It is often cooler in the shade. (B9)

shelter A shelter is a safe place to live. A nest is shelter for a bird. (A31)

skin Skin covers the bodies of animals. Skin can be protected by hair, feathers, or scales. (A24)

sleep Sleep is a period of rest. When you sleep, your body refreshes itself. (E27)

snack A snack is food you eat between meals. Fruits are healthful snacks. Potato chips and candy are unhealthful snacks. (E14)

spring Spring is a season of the year. It comes after winter. In spring, many plants begin to grow. (B29)

stem A stem is a plant part. Water and food move through stems. Some stems are hard. (A9)

stream A stream is a narrow path of flowing water. Streams are smaller than rivers. (D31)

strong wind A wind that blows fast and hard. A strong wind will blow paper down the street. (B19)

summer Summer is the season that comes after spring. It is the warmest season. Days are longer in the summer. (B29)

temperature The measure of heat in an object. Temperature is measured using a thermometer. (B5)

temporary magnet A magnet that works only for a short time. A temporary magnet can be made by stroking a metal object with a magnet. (C28)

topsoil Topsoil is the top part of soil. It is the part of soil in which most plants grow. Worms live in topsoil. (D5)

water vapor Water vapor is water that is in the form of a gas. You cannot see water vapor. (B22)

weather Weather is what the air outside is like. Weather changes from day to day. (B4)

winter Winter is the season that comes after autumn. It is the coldest of the four seasons. Days are short in the winter. (B29)

INDEX

W

CREDITS

Cover: *Photography:* Jade Albert; *Photography Production:* Picture It Corporation; *Illustration:* Mary Thelen.

ILLUSTRATORS
UNIT A A4–A5: Dave Schweitzer. **A12–A13:** *borders* Anne Feiza. **A16–A17:** Bob Pepper. **A30–A33:** Patrick Gnan. **A36–A37:** Randy Hamblin. **A42:** Sharon Hawkins Vargo.

UNIT B B8–B9: John Jones. **B28–B29:** Ellen Appleby. **B42:** Sharon Hawkins Vargo.

UNIT C C18–C19: *background* Julie Carpenter; *wooden toys* Jerry Pavey. **C34:** Sharon Hawkins Vargo.

UNIT D D4–D5: Robert Roper. **D34–D35:** Susan Hunt Yule. **D40:** Sharon Hawkins Vargo.

UNIT E E4–E7: Dan Brawner. **E26–E27:** Barbara Gray. **E30–E31:** Jenny Campbell. **E36:** Sharon Hawkins Vargo.

GLOSSARY: Sharon Hawkins Vargo.

PHOTOGRAPHS
All photographs by Silver Burdett Ginn (SBG) unless otherwise noted.

UNIT A A8: *t.* Walter Chandoha; *m.* © Hans Reinhard/Photo Researchers, Inc.; *b.* Hans Pfletschinger/Peter Arnold. **A8–A9:** George Hunter/Tony Stone Images. **A12:** *l.* Arthur R. Hill/Visuals Unlimited; *r.* Fritz Polking GDT/Peter Arnold. **A13:** *l.* Ron Watts/Westlight; *r.* Richard Kolar/Earth Scenes. **A20–A21:** Stephen Dalton/Animals Animals. **A24:** *t.l.* © Stephen Collins/Photo Researchers, Inc.; *t.r.* © Thomas Martin/Photo Researchers, Inc.; *b.l.* Darryll Schiff/Tony Stone Images; *b.r.* Zefa Germany/The Stock Market. **A25:** *t.l.* John M. Roberts/The Stock Market; *t.r., b.l.* Thomas Kitchin/Tom Stack & Associates; *b.r.* Brian Parker/Tom Stack & Associates. **A26:** *t.l.* Stephen J. Krasemann/ Allstock/Tony Stone Images; *t.r.* © Bill Dyer/Photo Researchers, Inc.; *b.l.* Miriam Austerman/Animals Animals; *b.r.* Zig Leszcynski/Animals Animals. **A27:** *b.l.* © Tim Davis/Photo Researchers, Inc.; *b.r.* Brian Parker/Tom Stack & Associates. **A36:** Art Wolfe/Tony Stone Images. **A37:** S. Purdy Matthews/Tony Stone Images. **A40:** *t.l.* Sue Streeter/Tony Stone Images; *t.r.* Charles Krebs/Tony Stone Images; *b.l.* Mike Bacon/Tom Stack & Associates; *b.r.* © Gregory Dimijian/Photo Researchers, Inc. **A41:** *t.l.* Jeanne Drake/Tony Stone Images; *t.r.* © Jim Steinberg/Photo Researchers, Inc.; *b.l.* © Nick Bergkessel/Photo Researchers, Inc.; *b.r.* Fritz Prenzel/Tony Stone Images.

UNIT B B4–B5: Grant Huntington for SBG. **B12–B13:** Tony Freeman/PhotoEdit. **B16–B19:** Oldrich Karasek/ Tony Stone Images. **B19:** *t.* Tony Freeman/PhotoEdit; *m.* Chris Hackett/The Image Bank; *b.* Wes Thompson/The Stock Market. **B22–B25:** Richard Hutchings for SBG. **B32:** Tony Freeman/PhotoEdit. **B33:** Bob Skjold/PhotoEdit. **B36:** Hans Reinhard/Bruce Coleman. **B37:** Wayne Lankinen/Bruce Coleman. **B40–B41:** Eric A. Soder/Tom Stack & Associates. **B43:** Richard Hutchings/PhotoEdit.

UNIT C C8–C9: Ken Karp for SBG. **C33:** *t.* Grant Huntington for SBG.

UNIT D D14–D15: Patti McConville/The Image Bank. **D22:** *t.l., t.r.* Jerry Jacka; *b.* David R. Frazier. **D23:** David R. Frazier. **D26–D27, D30:** Superstock. **D30–D31:** Craig Tuttle/The Stock Market. **D31:** Tim Davis/Tony Stone Images. **D38–D39:** Bill Field.

UNIT E E10, E11: Steven Mark Needham/Envision. **E10–E11:** Rich Osentaski/Envision. **E18–E19:** Robert Daemmrich Photography. **E19:** Tim Davis. **E37:** © Catherine Ursillo/Photo Researchers, Inc.